ARCHIMATE® 3.0.1 – A POCKET GUIDE

The Open Group Publications available from Van Haren Publishing

The TOGAF Series:
TOGAF® Version 9.1
TOGAF® Version 9.1 – A Pocket Guide
TOGAF® 9 Foundation Study Guide, 3rd Edition
TOGAF® 9 Certified Study Guide, 3rd Edition

The Open Group Series:
The IT4IT™ Reference Architecture, Version 2.1
IT4IT™ for Managing the Business of IT – A Management Guide
IT4IT™ Foundation Study Guide, 2nd edition
The IT4IT™ Reference Architecture, Version 2.1 – A Pocket Guide
Cloud Computing for Business – The Open Group Guide
ArchiMate® 3.0.1 – A Pocket Guide
ArchiMate® 2 Certification – Study Guide
ArchiMate® 3.0.1 Specification

The Open Group Security Series:
O-TTPS - A Management Guide
Open Information Security Management Maturity Model (O-ISM3)
Open Enterprise Security Architecture (O-ESA)
Risk Management – The Open Group Guide
The Open FAIR™ Body of Knowledge – A Pocket Guide

All titles are available to purchase from:
www.opengroup.org
www.vanharen.net
and also many international and online distributors.

ArchiMate® 3.0.1

A POCKET GUIDE

Title:	ArchiMate® 3.0.1 – A Pocket Guide
Series:	The Open Group Series
A Publication of:	The Open Group
Author:	Andrew Josey et al.
Publisher:	Van Haren Publishing, Zaltbommel, www.vanharen.net
ISBN hard copy:	978 94 018 0231 4
ISBN eBook:	978 94 018 0232 1
ISBN ePuB:	978 94 018 0233 8
Edition:	First edition, first impression, March 2012
	Second edition, first impression, December 2013
	Third edition, first impression, July 2016
	Fourth edition, first impression, September 2017
Layout and cover design:	Coco Bookmedia, Amersfoort – NL
Copyright:	© The Open Group 2012, 2013, 2017 All rights reserved

ArchiMate® 3.0.1
A Pocket Guide
Document Number: G163

Published by The Open Group

Comments relating to the material contained in this document may be submitted to:

The Open Group
Apex Plaza
Forbury Road
Reading
Berkshire, RG1 1AX
United Kingdom

or by electronic mail to: ogspecs@opengroup.org

Contents

Preface

This Document

This is the Pocket Guide to the ArchiMate® 3.0.1 Specification, an Open Group Standard. It is intended to help architects by providing a reference for the ArchiMate graphical modeling language and also assist managers in understanding the basics of the ArchiMate language. It is organized as follows:

- Chapter 1 provides a high-level introduction to the ArchiMate Specification and its relationship to Enterprise Architecture
- Chapter 2 describes the high-level structure of the ArchiMate language, including an introduction to layering, and the ArchiMate Framework
- Chapter 3 describes the Generic Metamodel for the language
- Chapter 4 describes the relationships that the ArchiMate language includes to model the links between elements
- Chapter 5 describes the Motivation Elements, which includes concepts such as goal, principle, and requirement
- Chapter 6 describes the Strategy Elements, which includes concepts such as resource, capability, and course of action
- Chapter 7 describes the Business Layer, which includes the modeling concepts relevant in the business domain
- Chapter 8 describes the Application Layer, which includes modeling concepts relevant for software applications
- Chapter 9 describes the Technology Layer, which includes modeling concepts relevant for system software applications and infrastructure
- Chapter 10 describes the Physical Elements, which include concepts relevant for the modeling of physical concepts like machines and physical installations
- Chapter 11 describes the relationships between different layers of the language
- Chapter 12 describes the Implementation and Migration Elements, which include concepts to support modeling Enterprise Architecture-enabled transformation

- Chapter 13 introduces the concept of ArchiMate Viewpoints
- Appendix A contains a summary of the changes from ArchiMate Version 2.1 to ArchiMate Version 3.0
- A Glossary of terms and Index are provided

The audience for this document is:
- Enterprise architects, business architects, IT architects, application architects, data architects, software architects, systems architects, solutions architects, infrastructure architects, process architects, domain architects, product managers, operational managers, and senior managers seeking a first introduction to the ArchiMate modeling language

After reading this document, the reader seeking further information should refer to the ArchiMate documentation[1] available online at www.opengroup.org/archimate.

Conventions Used in this Document

The following conventions are used throughout this document in order to help identify important information and avoid confusion over the intended meaning:

- Ellipsis (…)
  Indicates a continuation; such as an incomplete list of example items, or a continuation from preceding text.
- **Bold**
  Used to highlight specific terms.
- *Italics*
  Used for emphasis. May also refer to other external documents.

---

1   ArchiMate® 3.0.1 Specification, Open Group Standard (C179), published by The Open Group, August 2017; refer to: www.opengroup.org/bookstore/catalog/c179.htm.

In addition to typographical conventions, the following convention is used to highlight segments of text:

 A Note box is used to highlight useful or interesting information.

About The Open Group

The Open Group is a global consortium that enables the achievement of business objectives through IT standards. With more than 500 member organizations, The Open Group has a diverse membership that spans all sectors of the IT community – customers, systems and solutions suppliers, tool vendors, integrators, and consultants, as well as academics and researchers – to:

- Capture, understand, and address current and emerging requirements, and establish policies and share best practices
- Facilitate interoperability, develop consensus, and evolve and integrate specifications and open source technologies
- Operate the industry's premier certification service

Further information on The Open Group is available at www.opengroup.org.

Trademarks

About the Authors

Andrew Josey

Andrew Josey is VP Standards and Certification, overseeing all certification and testing programs of The Open Group. He also manages the Standards Process for The Open Group. Since joining the company in 1996, Andrew has been closely involved with the standards development, certification, and testing activities of The Open Group. He has led many standards development projects including specification and certification development for the ArchiMate®, TOGAF®, IT4IT™, POSIX®, and UNIX® programs.

He is a member of the IEEE, USENIX, UKUUG, and the Association of Enterprise Architects (AEA). He holds an MSc in Computer Science from University College London.

Marc Lankhorst, BiZZdesign

Marc Lankhorst is Managing Consultant and Business Design Evangelist at BiZZdesign. He is responsible for market development, consulting, and coaching on digital business design and Enterprise Architecture, and spreading the word on the ArchiMate modeling language for EA. His expertise and interests range from Enterprise Architecture and business process management to agile methods, portfolio management, and digital business design. Previously, Marc was a Senior Member of Scientific Staff at Novay (formerly Telematica Instituut), where he managed the collaborative R&D project that developed the initial version of the ArchiMate language. He leads the core team of The Open Group ArchiMate Forum that has defined the new version of the standard.

Iver Band, Cambia Health Solutions

Iver Band is a practicing Enterprise Architect and a developer and communicator of Enterprise Architecture standards and methods. At Cambia Health Solutions, he has guided initiatives focusing on provider systems, web and mobile experiences, and architecture methods and tools. He is currently focused on solutions that provide information about healthcare consumers and groups. Iver is also the elected Vice-Chair of the ArchiMate Forum. He has led development of several Open Group White Papers and contributed to the second and third major versions of the ArchiMate language. He holds TOGAF 9 and ArchiMate 3 Practitioner certifications from The Open Group. He is a Certified Information Systems Security Professional (CISSP), a Certified Information Professional, an AHIP Information Technology Professional, and a Prosci Certified Change Consultant.

Henk Jonkers, BiZZdesign
Henk Jonkers is a Senior Research Consultant, involved in BiZZdesign's innovations in the areas of Enterprise Architecture and engineering. He participates in multi-party research projects, contributes to training courses, and performs consultancy assignments. Previously, as a member of scientific staff at the Telematica Instituut, he was involved in research projects on business process modeling and analysis, EA, SOA, and model-driven development. He was one of the main developers of the ArchiMate language and an author of the ArchiMate 1.0, 2.1, and 3.0 Specifications, and is actively involved in the activities of The Open Group ArchiMate Forum.

Dick Quartel, BiZZdesign
Dick Quartel is a Senior Research Consultant at BiZZdesign. In this role he contributes to the development and improvement of BiZZdesign's products and services, is involved in research projects, supervises MSc students and interns, and performs consultancy assignments. In addition, he is an author of many scientific and professional publications, and an author of the ArchiMate 2.1 and 3.0 Specifications. Previously, he worked as a Senior Researcher at Novay (formerly Telematica Instituut), where he acted as researcher and project manager and contributed to the definition and acquisition of research projects. As an Assistant Professor at the University of Twente, he worked in the areas of distributed systems design, protocol design and implementation, and middleware systems.

Steve Else, EA Principals

Steve Else is the CEO of EA Principals, a Gold Member of The Open Group. Steve is certified in the TOGAF 8, TOGAF 9, ArchiMate 3, Open FAIR, and IT4IT certification programs. A former Air Force pilot with a rating to fly the Boeing 717 and Lear Jet commercially, Steve became an Enterprise Architect about 20 years ago while helping direct the US Air Force Business Transformation initiative. He has been Chief Architect at numerous organizations, done consulting at uniquely challenging organizations, such as the United Nations and Fannie Mae, and taught EA to thousands of students over 10 years. He has also written two books on the TOGAF framework, along with one on Organization Theory and the Transformation of Large, Complex Organizations.

Acknowledgements

The Open Group gratefully acknowledges:

- Past and present members of The Open Group ArchiMate Forum for developing the ArchiMate Standard.
- The following reviewers of this document:
  - Peter Bates
  - Sonia Gonzalez
  - Dave Hornford
  - Russel Jones
  - Jean-Baptiste Sarrodie

Chapter 1
Introduction

This chapter provides an introduction to the ArchiMate Specification, an Open Group Standard.

Topics addressed in this chapter include:
- An introduction to the ArchiMate Specification
- A brief overview of the ArchiMate Specification
- The ArchiMate language and its relationship to Enterprise Architecture and the TOGAF Standard

1.1 Introduction to the ArchiMate Specification

The ArchiMate Specification, an Open Group Standard, is an open and independent modeling language for Enterprise Architecture that is supported by different tool vendors and consulting firms. The ArchiMate language enables Enterprise Architects to describe, analyze, and visualize the relationships among architecture domains in an unambiguous way.

Just as an architectural drawing in classical building architecture describes the various aspects of the construction and use of a building, the ArchiMate Specification offers a common language for describing the construction and operation of business processes, organizational structures, information flows, IT systems, and technical and physical infrastructure. This insight helps stakeholders to design, assess, and communicate the consequences of decisions and changes within and between these architecture domains.

This document is the Pocket Guide to the ArchiMate 3.0.1 Specification, referred to simply as the "ArchiMate Specification" within this document. The ArchiMate 3.0 Specification was first published as an Open Group Standard in June 2016. A set of corrections was published in August 2017, and incorporated into the specification to become the ArchiMate 3.0.1 Specification. New features included in the major update include elements for modeling the enterprise at a strategic level, such as capability, resource, and outcome. It also includes support to model the physical world of materials and equipment. Furthermore, the consistency and structure of the language have been improved, definitions have been aligned with other standards, and its usability has been enhanced in various other ways.

Development of the ArchiMate Language
The ArchiMate language was created in the period 2002-2004 in the Netherlands by a project team from the Telematica Instituut in co-operation with several partners from government, industry, and academia, including Ordina, Radboud Universiteit Nijmegen, the Leiden Institute for Advanced Computer Science (LIACS), and the Centrum Wiskunde & Informatica (CWI). The development included tests in organizations such as ABN AMRO, the Dutch Tax and Customs Administration, and the Stichting Pensioenfonds ABP.

In 2008, the ownership and stewardship of the ArchiMate language was transferred from the ArchiMate Foundation to The Open Group. Since 2009, The Open Group ArchiMate Forum has developed successive versions and published them on The Open Group public website.

1.2 ArchiMate Specification Overview

The ArchiMate Specification is The Open Group Standard for the ArchiMate architecture modeling language. It contains the formal definition of the visual design language.

The contents of the specification include the following:

- The introduction, including the objectives, overview, conformance requirements, normative references, and terminology
- Definitions of the general terms used in the specification
- The structure of the modeling language
- The generic metamodel of the language
- The relationships in the language

- A detailed breakdown of the modeling framework covering the motivation elements, strategy elements, the three layers (Business/Application/Technology), and the physical elements
- Cross-layer dependencies and alignment, and relationships within the framework
- Implementation and migration elements for expressing the implementation and migration aspects of an architecture
- The concepts of stakeholders, viewpoints, and views, and also the ArchiMate viewpoint mechanism
- Mechanisms for customizing the language for specialized or domain-specific purposes
- Notation overviews and summaries
- Informative descriptions of the relationship of the ArchiMate language to other standards, including the TOGAF framework, Business Process Modeling Notation (BPMN), Unified Modeling Language (UML), and Business Motivation Model (BMM)

The ArchiMate 3.0.1 Specification is the latest version of the specification and is an evolution from the ArchiMate 2.1 and earlier.

1.3 The ArchiMate Language and Enterprise Architecture

The role of the ArchiMate Specification is to provide a graphical language for the representation of Enterprise Architectures over time (i.e., including strategic, transformation, and migration planning), as well as the motivation and rationale for the architecture. The ArchiMate modeling language provides a uniform representation for diagrams that describe Enterprise Architectures, and offers an integrated approach to describe and visualize the different architecture domains together with their underlying relations and dependencies.

The design of the ArchiMate language started from a set of relatively generic concepts (objects and relations), which have been specialized for application at the different architectural layers for an Enterprise

Architecture. The most important design restriction on the ArchiMate language is that it has been explicitly designed to be as compact as possible, yet still usable for most Enterprise Architecture modeling tasks. In the interest of simplicity of learning and use, the language has been limited to the concepts that suffice for modeling the proverbial 80% of practical cases.

1.3.1 The ArchiMate Language and the TOGAF ADM

The ArchiMate language consists of the ArchiMate core language, that includes the Business, Application, and Technology layers, and elements to model the Strategy and Motivation for an architecture, as well as its Implementation and Migration. Figure 1 shows a simplified mapping of how the ArchiMate language can be used in relation to the phases of the TOGAF ADM.

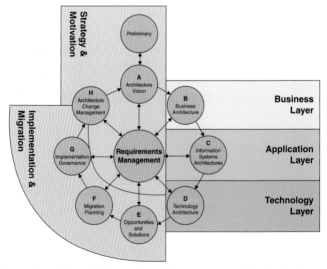

Figure 1: The Relationship between the ArchiMate Language and the TOGAF ADM

The Business, Application, and Technology layers support the description of the architecture domains defined by the TOGAF framework (business, information systems, and technology, as well as their inter-relationships).

The strategy and motivation elements in the ArchiMate language can be used to support the Requirements Management, Preliminary Phase, and Architecture Vision phases of the TOGAF ADM, which establish the high-level business goals, architecture principles, and initial business requirements. They are also relevant to the Architecture Change Management phase of the TOGAF ADM, since the phase deals with changing requirements. Although not shown in the figure, it should be noted that these elements could also be used in other ADM phases, such as Phases B, C, and D.

The implementation and migration elements of the ArchiMate language support the implementation and migration of architectures through the Opportunities and Solutions, Migration Planning, and Implementation Governance phases of the TOGAF ADM.

Chapter 2
Language Structure

This chapter describes the construction of the ArchiMate language.
Topics addressed in this chapter include:

- The top-level language structure
- Layering
- The ArchiMate Framework

2.1 Top-Level Language Structure

Figure 2 outlines the top-level hierarchical structure of the language:

- A model is a collection of concepts. A concept is an element, a relationship, or a relationship connector
- An element is a behavior element, a structure element, a motivation element, or a composite element

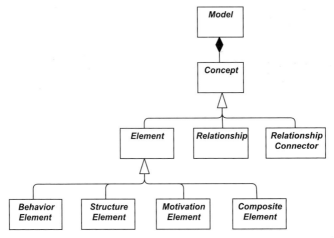

Figure 2: Top-Level Hierarchy of ArchiMate Concepts

Figure 2 describes *abstract* concepts; they are not intended to be used directly in models. To signify this, they are depicted in white with labels in italics. Further note that implementation and migration elements are instances of core elements.

2.2 Layering of the ArchiMate Language

The ArchiMate core language defines a structure of generic elements and their relationships, which can be specialized in different layers. Three layers are defined within the ArchiMate core language as follows:

1. The *Business Layer* depicts business services offered to customers, which are realized in the organization by business processes performed by business actors.
2. The *Application Layer* depicts application services that support the business, and the applications that realize them.
3. The *Technology Layer* depicts technology services such as processing, storage, and communication services needed to run the applications, and the computer and communication hardware and system software that realize those services. Physical elements are added for modeling physical equipment, materials, and distribution networks to this layer.

The general structure of models within the different layers is similar. The same types of elements and relationships are used, although their exact nature and granularity differ.

In alignment with service-orientation, the most important relationship between layers is formed by "serving" relationships, which show how the elements in one layer are served by the services of other layers. (Note, however, that services need not only serve elements in another layer, but also can serve elements in the same layer.) A second type of link is formed by realization relationships: elements in lower layers may realize comparable elements in higher layers; e.g., a "data object" (Application Layer) may realize a "business object" (Business Layer); or an "artifact" (Technology Layer) may realize either a "data object" or an "application component" (Application Layer).

2.3 Use of Colors and Notational Cues

In the metamodel pictures within this Pocket Guide (e.g., Figure 30) and the ArchiMate 3.0.1 Specification, shades of grey are used to distinguish elements belonging to the different aspects of the ArchiMate Framework, as follows:

- White for abstract (i.e., non-instantiable) concepts
- Light grey for passive structures
- Medium grey for behavior
- Dark grey for active structures

In ArchiMate models, there are no formal semantics assigned to colors and the use of color is left to the modeler. However, they can be used freely to stress certain aspects in models. For instance, in many of the example models presented in this Guide, colors are used to distinguish between the layers of the ArchiMate Core Framework (see Section 2.4), as follows:

- Yellow for the Business Layer
- Blue for the Application Layer
- Green for the Technology Layer

They can also be used for visual emphasis.

In addition to the colors, other notational cues can be used to distinguish between the layers of the framework. A letter 'M', 'S', 'B', 'A', 'T', 'P', or 'I' in the top-left corner of an element can be used to denote a Motivation, Strategy, Business, Application, Technology, Physical, or Implementation & Migration element, respectively.

The standard notation also uses a convention with the shape of the corners of its symbols for different element types, as follows:

- Square corners are used to denote structure elements (see Section 3.1.1)
- Round corners are used to denote behavior elements (see Section 3.1.2)

- Diagonal corners are used to denote motivation elements
  (see Section 3.3)

2.4 The ArchiMate Core Framework

The aspects of the core, as defined by the three types of element at the bottom of Figure 2, combined with the layers identified in the previous section, make up a framework of nine cells, as illustrated in Figure 3. This is known as the ArchiMate Core Framework.

It is important to understand that the classification of elements based on aspects and layers is only a global one. It is impossible to define a strict boundary between the aspects and layers because elements that link the different aspects and layers play a central role in a coherent architectural description. For example, (business) functions and (business) roles serve as intermediary elements between "purely behavioral" elements and "purely structural" elements, and it may depend on the context whether a certain piece of software is considered to be part of the Application Layer or the Technology Layer.

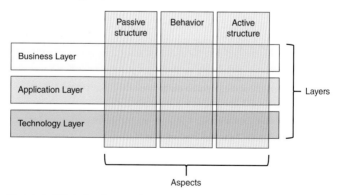

Figure 3: ArchiMate Core Framework

The structure of the framework allows for modeling of the enterprise from different viewpoints, where the position within the cells highlights the concerns of the stakeholder. A stakeholder typically can have concerns that cover multiple cells.

The dimensions of the framework are as follows:
- Layers: The three levels at which an enterprise can be modeled in the ArchiMate language – Business, Application, and Technology (as described in Section 2.2).
- Aspects:
  - The *Active Structure aspect*, which represents the structural elements (the business actors, application components, and devices that display actual behavior; i.e., the "subjects" of activity).
  - The *Behavior aspect*, which represents the behavior (processes, functions, events, and services) performed by the actors. Structural elements are assigned to behavioral elements, to show who or what displays the behavior.
  - The *Passive Structure aspect*, which represents the objects on which behavior is performed. These are usually information objects in the Business Layer and data objects in the Application Layer, but they may also be used to represent physical objects.

A composite element, as shown in Figure 2, is an element that does not necessarily fit in a single aspect (column) of the framework, but may combine two or more aspects.

 Note that the ArchiMate language does not require the modeler to use any particular layout such as the structure of this framework; it is merely a categorization of the language elements.

2.5 Full Framework
The full ArchiMate language specification adds a number of layers and an aspect to the framework. The strategy elements (see Chapter 6)

include elements for capability, resource, and course of action. The
physical elements (see Chapter 10) are added to the Technology Layer
for modeling physical facilities and equipment, distribution networks,
and materials. The motivation aspect is introduced at a generic
level in the next chapter and described in detail in Chapter 5. The
implementation and migration elements are described in Chapter 11.
The resulting full ArchiMate Framework is shown in Figure 4.

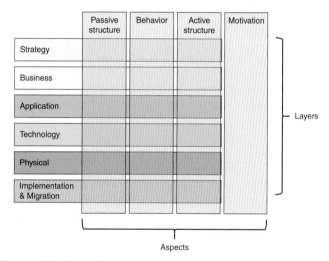

Figure 4: Full ArchiMate Framework

Information Modeling

The ArchiMate language does not define a specific layer for
information; however, elements from the passive structure aspect
(e.g., business objects, data objects, and technology objects) are
used to represent information entities. Information modeling is
supported across the different ArchiMate layers.

Chapter 3
Generic Metamodel

This chapter describes the ArchiMate generic metamodel that defines the full structure of the language.

3.1 Behavior and Structure Elements

The main hierarchy of behavior and structure elements of the ArchiMate language is presented in the metamodel fragment of Figure 5. It defines these elements in a generic, layer-independent way.

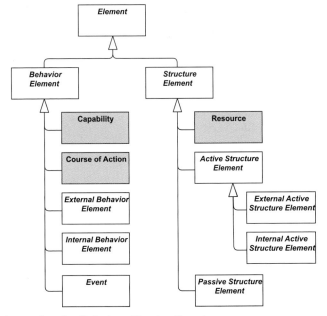

Figure 5: Hierarchy of Behavior and Structure Elements

This generic metamodel fragment consists of two main types of elements: *structure* ('nouns') and *behavior* elements ('verbs').

Structure elements are the strategic element *resource*, and structural elements, which are subdivided into *active structure* elements and *passive structure* elements. Active structure elements can be further subdivided into *external* active structure elements (also called *interfaces*) and *internal* active structure elements.

Behavior elements are the strategic elements *course of action* and *capability*, and behavioral elements which can be subdivided into *internal behavior* elements, *external behavior* elements (also called *services*), and *events*.

These three aspects – active structure, behavior, and passive structure – have been inspired by natural language, where a sentence has a subject (active structure), a verb (behavior), and an object (passive structure).

Figure 6 specifies the main relationships between the behavior and structure elements defined above. In this and other metamodel figures, the label of a relationship signifies the role of the source element in the relationship; e.g., a service serves an internal behavior element.

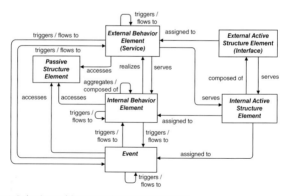

Figure 6: Behavior and Structure Elements Metamodel

3.1.1 Active Structure Elements

Active structure elements are the subjects that can perform behavior.
These can be subdivided into internal active structure elements – i.e.,
the business actors, application components, nodes, etc., that realize this
behavior – and external active structure elements – i.e., the interfaces
that expose this behavior to the environment. An interface provides an
external view on the service provider and hides its internal structure.

> An internal active structure element represents an entity that is
> capable of performing behavior.
>
> An external active structure element, called an interface, represents
> a point of access where one or more services are provided to the
> environment.

Active structure elements are denoted using boxes with square corners
and an icon in the upper-right corner, or by the icon on its own.

Figure 7: Generic Active Structure Elements Notation

3.1.2 Behavior Elements

Behavior elements represent the dynamic aspects of the enterprise.
Similar to active structure elements, behavior elements can be subdivided
into *internal* behavior elements and *external* behavior elements; i.e., the
services that are exposed to the environment.

> An internal behavior element represents a unit of activity performed by one or more active structure elements.
>
> An external behavior element, called a service, represents an explicitly defined exposed behavior.

Behavior elements are denoted in the standard iconography using boxes with round corners and an icon in the upper-right corner, or by the icon on its own.

Figure 8: Generic Behavior Elements Notation

In addition to this, a third type of behavior element is defined to denote an event that can occur; for example, to signal a state change.

> An event is a behavior element that denotes a state change.

An event may have a time attribute that indicates the moment or moments at which the event happens. For example, this can be used to model time schedules.

Figure 9: Generic Event Notation

3.1.3 Passive Structure Elements

Passive structure elements can be accessed by behavior elements.

> A passive structure element is a structural element that cannot
> perform behavior. Active structure elements can perform behavior on
> passive structure elements.

Passive structure elements are often information or data objects, but they
can also represent physical objects.

Figure 10: Generic Passive Structure Element Notation

3.2 Specializations of Structure and Behavior Elements

Going one level deeper in the structure of the language, the collective
nature of a behavior can be made either implicit (several active structure
elements assigned to the same internal behavior) or explicit through the
use of a collective internal behavior (interaction) that is performed by
(a collaboration of) multiple active structure elements.

> A collaboration is an aggregate of two or more active structure
> elements, working together to perform some collective behavior.

This collective internal behavior can be modeled as an interaction.

> An interaction is a unit of collective behavior performed by
> (a collaboration of) two or more active structure elements.

Figure 11: Generic Collaboration and Interaction Notation

Furthermore, for individual internal behavior elements, a distinction is made between processes and functions.

A process represents a sequence of behaviors that achieves a specific outcome.

A function represents a collection of behavior based on specific criteria, such as required resources, competences, or location.

Figure 12: Generic Process and Function Notation

The specializations of core elements are summarized in Figure 13. Within each layer, it is permitted to use composition and aggregation relationships between processes, functions, and interactions; e.g., a process can be composed of other processes, functions, and/or interactions.

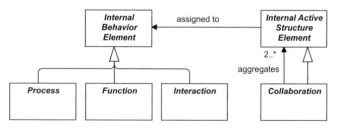

Figure 13: Specializations of Core Elements

3.3 Motivation Elements

Several *motivation elements* are included in the language: stakeholder, value, meaning, driver, assessment, goal, outcome, principle, and requirement, which in turn has constraint as a subtype. In this section, the generic motivation element is introduced. The more specific motivation elements are described in Chapter 5.

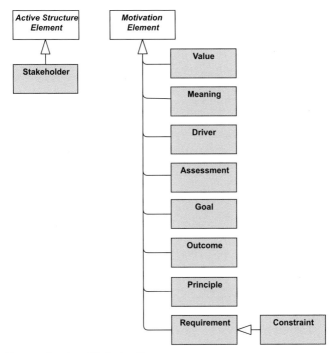

Figure 14: Overview of Motivation Elements

The motivation elements address the way the Enterprise Architecture is aligned to its context, as described by these intentions.

A motivation element is an element that provides the context of or reason behind the architecture of an enterprise.

Figure 15: Generic Motivation Element Notation

Motivation elements are usually denoted using boxes with diagonal corners.

3.4 Strategy Elements

Next to the motivation elements described in the previous section, the language also includes a number of *strategy elements*, notably capability, resource, and course of action, as exhibited in Figure 5. These are defined as specializations of the generic behavior and structure elements and are defined in more detail in Chapter 6.

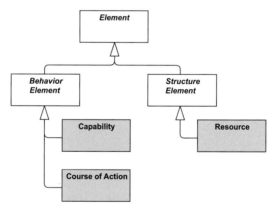

Figure 16: Strategy Elements

3.5 Composite Elements

Composite elements consist of other concepts, possibly from multiple aspects or layers of the language. Grouping and location are generic composite elements (see Figure 17). Composite elements can themselves aggregate or compose other composite elements.

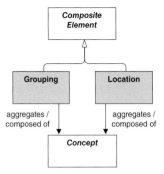

Figure 17: Composite Elements

3.5.1 Grouping

> The grouping element aggregates or composes concepts that belong together based on some common characteristic.

The grouping element is used to aggregate or compose an arbitrary group of concepts, which can be elements and/or relationships of the same or of different types. An aggregation or composition relationship is used to link the grouping element to the grouped concepts.

Figure 18: Grouping Notation

Concepts may be aggregated by multiple (overlapping) groups.

3.5.2 Location

> A location is a place or position where structure elements can be located or behavior can be performed.

The location element is used to model the places where (active and passive) structure elements, such as business actors, application components, and devices, are located. This is modeled by means of an aggregation relationship from a location to structure element. A location can also aggregate a behavior element, to indicate where the behavior is performed.

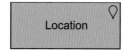

Figure 19: Location Notation

Chapter 4
Relationships

This chapter describes the relationships that the ArchiMate language includes to model the links between objects, concepts, and elements. Each of the relationships can connect a predefined set of source and target concepts – in most cases elements, but in a few cases also other relationships. Many of these relationships are 'overloaded'; i.e., their exact meaning differs depending on the source and destination concepts that they connect.

The relationships in the ArchiMate language are classified in four ways:
- **Structural**, which model the static construction or composition of concepts of the same or different types
- **Dependency,** which model how elements are used to support other elements

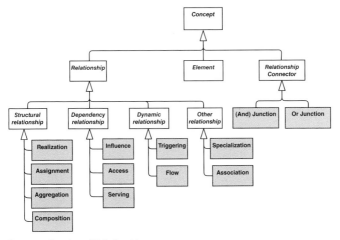

Figure 20: Overview of Relationships

- **Dynamic**, which are used to model behavioral dependencies between elements
- **Other**, which do not fall into one of the above categories

These are summarized in Table 1.

Relationships to Other Relationships
It is permitted to have relationships to other relationships in some cases; e.g., to associate objects with flows or aggregate relationships within plateaus.

4.1 Structural Relationships

Table 1: Structural Relationships

Structural Relationships		Notation
Composition	Indicates that an element consists of one or more other concepts. A composition relationship is always allowed between two instances of the same element type. The usual interpretation of a composition relationship is that the whole or part of the source element is composed of the whole of the target element. The entity at the end with the diamond is the parent of the entity on the other end (the child).	◆———

Structural Relationships		Notation
Aggregation	Indicates that an element consists of one or more other concepts. An aggregation relationship is always allowed between two instances of the same element type. The usual interpretation of an aggregation relationship is that the whole or part of the source element aggregates the whole of the target element. The entity at the end with a diamond is considered to be the parent of the entity at the end without a diamond. An alternate notation is to nest elements.	◇———
Assignment	Expresses the allocation of responsibility, performance of behavior, or execution. The assignment relationship links active structure elements with units of behavior that are performed by them, business actors with business roles that are fulfilled by them, and nodes with technology objects. It always points from active structure to behavior, and from behavior to passive structure. The non-directional notation from the ArchiMate 2.1 Specification and before, which shows the black ball at both ends of the relationship, is still allowed but deprecated. The usual interpretation of an assignment relationship is that the whole or part of the source element is assigned the whole of the target element. This means that if, for example, two active structure elements are assigned to the same behavior element, either of them can perform the complete behavior. An alternate notation is to nest elements.	●——▶

Structural Relationships		Notation
Realization	Indicates that an entity plays a critical role in the creation, achievement, sustenance, or operation of a more abstract entity. Indicates that more abstract entities ("what" or "logical") are realized by means of more tangible entities (e.g., "how" or "physical", respectively). The usual interpretation of a realization relationship is that the whole or part of the source element realizes the whole of the target element. This means that if, for example, two internal behavior elements have a realization relationship to the same service, either of them can realize the complete service. The entity at the end without the arrow head realizes the entity at the end with an arrow head.	·············▷

4.2 Dependency Relationships

Table 2: Dependency Relationships

Dependency Relationships		Notation
Serving	Models that an element provides its functionality to another element. This represents a control dependency, denoted by a solid line. The serving relationship describes how the services or interfaces offered by a behavior or active structure element serve entities in their environment. This relationship is applied for both the behavior and active structure aspects. The entity at the end without the arrow head serves the entity at the end with the arrow head.	⟶

Dependency Relationships		Notation
Access	Models the ability of behavior and active structure elements to observe or act upon passive structure elements. This represents a *data* dependency, denoted by a dashed line. The access relationship indicates that a process, function, interaction, service, or event "does something" with a passive structure element; e.g., create a new object, read data from the object, write or modify the object data, or delete the object. The relationship can also be used to indicate that the object is just associated with the behavior; e.g., it models the information that comes with an event, or the information that is made available as part of a service. The arrow head, if present, indicates the direction of the flow of information.	·· ··> <··>
Influence	Models that an element affects the implementation or achievement of some motivation element. This is the weakest type of dependency, and is used to model how motivation elements are influenced by other elements.	+/- --------------->

 The Serving Relationship replaces Used By Relationship
Compared to the earlier versions of this standard, the name of the 'used by' relationship has been changed to 'serving', to better reflect its direction with an active verb: a service serves a user. The meaning of the relationship has not been altered. The 'used by' designation is still allowed but deprecated, and will be removed in a future version of the standard.

4.3 Dynamic Relationships

Table 3: Dynamic Relationships

Dynamic Relationships		Notation
Triggering	Describes a temporal or causal relationship between elements. The usual interpretation of a triggering relationship is that the source element should be completed before the target element can start, although weaker interpretations are also permitted.	⟶
Flow	Transfer from one element to another. This is used to model the flow of, for example, information, goods, or money between behavior elements.	⤍

4.4 Other Relationships

Table 4: Other Relationships

Other Relationships		Notation
Specialization	Indicates that an element is a particular kind of another element.	—▷
Association	Models an unspecified relationship, or one that is not represented by another ArchiMate relationship. An association relationship is always allowed between two elements, or between a relationship and an element.	—

Other Relationships		Notation
Junction	Used to connect relationships of the same type. A junction is not an actual relationship in the same sense as the other relationships, but rather a relationship connector. A junction may have multiple incoming relationships and one outgoing relationship, one incoming relationship and multiple outgoing relationships, or multiple incoming and outgoing relationships (the latter can be considered a shorthand of two subsequent junctions). A junction is used to explicitly express that several elements *together* participate in the relationship (*and* junction) or that one of the elements participates in the relationship (*or* junction).	● ○ (And) Junction Or Junction

4.5 Examples

4.5.1 Composition Relationship

The models below show the two ways to express that the Financial Processing function is composed of three sub-functions.

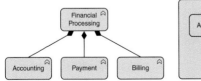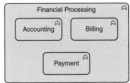

Example 1: Composition

4.5.2 Aggregation Relationship

The models below show two ways to express that the Customer File aggregates an Insurance Policy and Insurance Claim.

Example 2: Aggregation

4.5.3 Assignment Relationship

The model in the example below includes the two ways to express the assignment relationship. The Finance active structure element is assigned to the Transaction Processing function, and the Payment Interface is assigned to the Payment Service.

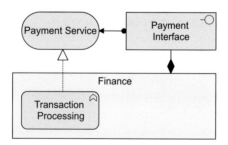

Example 3: Assignment

4.5.4 Realization Relationship

The model below illustrates two ways to use the realization
relationship. A Transaction Processing function realizes a Billing
Service; the Billing Data object is realized by the representation
Paper Invoice.

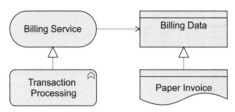

Example 4: Realization

4.5.5 Serving Relationship

The model below illustrates the serving relationship. The Payment
Interface serves the Customer, while the Payment Service serves the
Pay Invoices process of that customer.

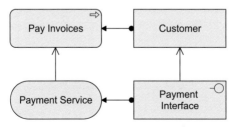

Example 5: Serving

4.5.6 Access Relationship

The model below illustrates the access relationship. The Create
Invoice sub-process writes/creates the Invoice object; the Send
Invoice sub-process reads that object.

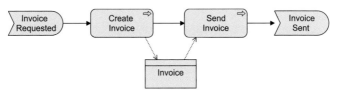

Example 6: Access

4.5.7 Influence Relationship

The model below illustrates the use of the influence relationship to
model the different effects of the same motivation element, Assign
Personal Assistant. This has a strongly positive influence on Reduce
Workload Of Employees, but a strongly negative influence on
Decrease Costs.

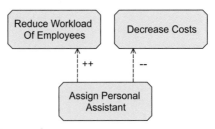

Example 7: Influence

4.5.8 Triggering Relationship

The model below illustrates the use of triggering relationships to model causal dependencies between (sub-)processes and/or events.

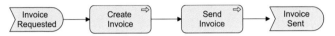

Example 8: Triggering

4.5.9 Flow Relationship

The model below shows a Claim Assessment function, which forwards decisions about the claims to the Claim Settlement function. In order to determine the order in which the claims should be assessed, Claim Assessment makes use of schedule information received from the Scheduling function.

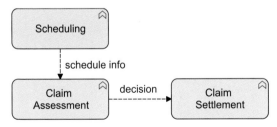

Example 9: Flow

4.5.10 Specialization Relationship

The model below illustrates the use of the specialization relationship
for a process. In this case the Take Out Travel Insurance and Take
Out Luggage Insurance processes are a specialization of a more
generic Take Out Insurance process.

Example 10: Specialization

4.5.11 Association Relationship

The model illustrates a number of uses of the association
relationship. It also shows an example of an association between
a flow relationship and a passive structure element, to indicate
the kind of information that is communicated between the two
functions.

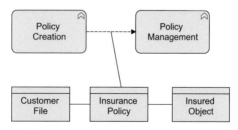

Example 11: Association

4.5.12 Junction

In the model below, the junction in the model is used to denote that the Sales and Finance functions together realize the Invoicing service.

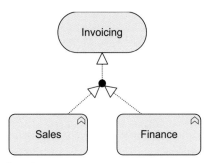

Example 12: (And) Junction

In the model below, the or junction is used to denote a choice: process Assess Request triggers either Accept Request or Reject Request. If the and junction were used instead, it would mean that Assess Request triggers both of the other processes.

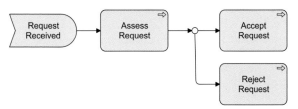

Example 13: Or Junction

4.6 Derivation Rules

This section describes the rules to derive indirect relationships between elements in a model, based on the modeled relationships. This makes it possible to abstract from intermediary elements that are not relevant to show in a certain model or view of the architecture, and is typically used to support impact analysis.

Applicability of Derived Relationships
Note that these derivation rules do not work on relationships with grouping, or between core elements and other elements such as motivation, strategy, or implementation and migration elements, with the exception of the realization and influence relationships.

4.6.1 Derivation Rule for Structural and Dependency Relationships

The structural and dependency relationships can be ordered by 'strength'. Structural relationships are 'stronger' than dependency relationships, and the relationships within these categories can also be ordered by strength:

- Influence (weakest)
- Access
- Serving
- Realization
- Assignment
- Aggregation
- Composition (strongest)

Part of the language definition is an abstraction rule that states that two relationships that join at an intermediate element can be combined and replaced by the weaker of the two.

If two structural or dependency relationships $r:R$ and $s:S$ are permitted between elements a, b, and c such that $r(a,b)$ and $s(b,c)$, then a structural relationship $t:T$ is also permitted, with $t(a,c)$ and type T being the weakest of R and S.

Transitively applying this property allows us to replace a 'chain' of structural relationships (with intermediate model elements) by the weakest structural relationship in the chain. Note that the resulting derived relationship can be valuable for impact analysis.

An example is shown in the figure below: assume that the goal is to omit the functions, sub-functions, and services from the model. In this case, an indirect serving relationship (the relationship labeled Derived Relationship (thick arrow on the right) can be derived from the Financial Application to the Invoicing and Collections process (from the chain assignment – composition – realization – serving).

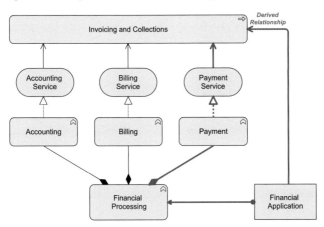

Example 14: Derived Structural and Dependency Relationship

4.6.2 Derivation Rules for Dynamic Relationships
For the two dynamic relationships, the following rules apply:
- If there is a flow relationship r from element a to element b, and a structural relationship from element c to element a, a flow relationship r can be derived from element c to element b

- If there is a flow relationship *r* from element *a* to element *b*, and a structural relationship from element *d* to element *b*, a flow relationship *r* can be derived from element *a* to element *d*

These rules can be applied repeatedly. Informally, this means that the begin and/or endpoint of a flow relationship can be transferred 'backward' in a chain of elements connected by structural relationships. The example below shows two of the possible flow relationships that can be derived with these rules, given a flow relationship between the two services.

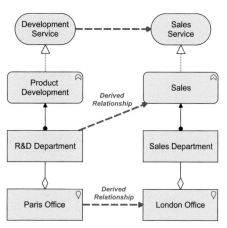

Example 15: Derived Flow Relationships

This rule also applies for a triggering relationship, but only in combination with an assignment relationship (not with other structural relationships):

- If there is a triggering relationship *r* from element *a* to element *b*, and an assignment relationship from element *c* to element *a*, a triggering relationship *r* can be derived from element *c* to element *b*

- If there is a triggering relationship *r* from element *a* to element *b*, and an assignment relationship from element *d* to element *b*, a triggering relationship *r* can be derived from element *a* to element *d*

Moreover, triggering relationships are *transitive*:
- If there is a triggering relationship from element *a* to element *b*, and a triggering relationship from element *b* to element *c*, a triggering relationship can be derived from element *a* to element *c*

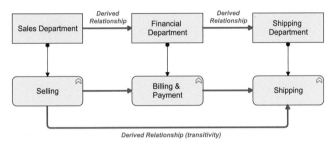

Example 16: Derived Triggering Relationships

Chapter 5
Motivation Elements

Motivation elements are used to model the motivations, or reasons, that guide the design or change of an Enterprise Architecture.

5.1 Motivation Elements Metamodel

Figure 21 gives an overview of the motivation elements and their relationships.

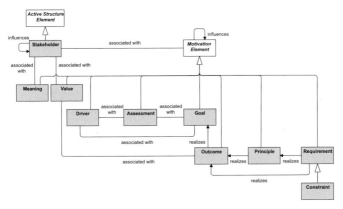

Figure 21: Motivation Elements Metamodel

5.2 Motivation Elements Summary

Table 5 gives an overview of the motivation elements, with their definitions.

Table 5: Motivation Elements

Element	Definition	Notation
Stakeholder	The role of an individual, team, or organization (or classes thereof) that represents their interests in the outcome of the architecture. In order to direct efforts to their interests and concerns, stakeholders change, set, and emphasize goals. Stakeholders may also influence each other. Examples of stakeholders are CxOs and key directors and managers in an organization, the board of directors, shareholders, customers, business and application architects, and external partners and regulators. The name of a stakeholder should preferably be a noun.	Stakeholder
Driver	An external or internal condition that motivates an organization to define its goals and implement the changes necessary to achieve them. Drivers may be internal, in which case they are usually associated with a stakeholder, and are often called "concerns". Drivers of change may also be external; e.g., economic changes or changing legislation. The name of a driver should preferably be a noun.	Driver

Element	Definition	Notation
Assessment	The result of an analysis of the state of affairs of the enterprise with respect to some driver. An assessment may reveal strengths, weaknesses, opportunities, or threats for some area of interest. These need to be addressed by adjusting existing goals or setting new ones. Strengths and weaknesses are internal to the organization. Opportunities and threats are external to the organization. The name of an assessment should be a noun or a short sentence.	Assessment
Goal	A high-level statement of intent, direction, or desired end state for an organization and its stakeholders. Goals are generally expressed using qualitative words; e.g., "increase", "improve", or "easier". Goals can also be decomposed.	Goal
Outcome	An end result that has been achieved. Outcomes are high-level, business-oriented results produced by capabilities of an organization. Outcome names should unambiguously identify end results that have been achieved in order to avoid confusion with actions or goals. Outcome names should consist of a noun identifying the end result followed by a past-tense verb or adjective indicating that the result has been achieved; e.g., "First-place ranking achieved" and "Key supplier partnerships in place".	Outcome

Element	Definition	Notation
Principle	A qualitative statement of intent that should be met by the architecture. Similar to requirements, principles define intended properties of systems. However, in contrast to requirements, principles are broader in scope and more abstract than requirements. A principle is motivated by some goal or driver. The name of a principle should be easily understood, whether with a word or two, or even a short sentence.	Principle
Requirement	A statement of need that must be met by the architecture. Requirements model the properties of these elements that are needed to achieve the "ends" that are modeled by the goals. In this respect, requirements represent the "means" to realize goals. The name of a requirement should be easily understood and is often a short sentence.	Requirement
Constraint	A factor that prevents or obstructs the realization of goals. In contrast to a requirement, a constraint does not prescribe some intended functionality of the system to be realized, but imposes a restriction on the way it operates or may be realized. The name of a constraint should be easily understood and is often a short sentence.	Constraint

Element	Definition	Notation
Meaning	The knowledge or expertise present in, or the interpretation given to, a core element in a particular context. A meaning represents the interpretation of an element of the architecture. In particular, this is used to describe the meaning of passive structure elements (for example, a document or message). The name of a meaning should be a noun or noun phrase.	Meaning
Value	The relative worth, utility, or importance of a core element or an outcome. A value can be associated with all core elements of an architecture, as well as with outcomes. It is recommended that the name of a value be expressed as an action or state that can be performed or reached.	Value

Value and Meaning moved from Business Layer to Motivation Elements
In earlier versions of this standard, the value and meaning concepts were present in the Business Layer of the ArchiMate core language.

5.3 Examples

5.3.1 Stakeholder, Driver, and Assessment

The stakeholder Chief Marketing Officer (CMO) is concerned with the driver Market Share, the stakeholder Chief Executive Officer (CEO) is concerned with the drivers Market Share and Profitability, and the stakeholder Chief Financial Officer (CFO) is concerned with the driver Profitability. The driver Profitability is composed of two other drivers: Revenue and Costs. Several assessments are associated with these drivers (e.g., the assessment Market Share Is Declining is associated with driver

Market Share), and assessments may influence each other in a positive or negative way (e.g., Market Share Is Declining results in Revenue Is Declining, which in turn results in Profitability Is Declining).

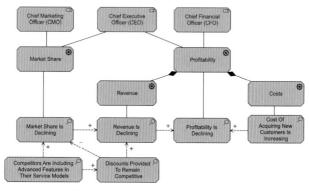

Example 17: Stakeholder, Driver, and Assessment

5.3.2 Goal, Outcome, Principle, Requirement, and Constraint

The goal Improve Profitability of Service Offering is realized by the outcome Increased Profit. This outcome is influenced positively by the outcomes Increased Revenue and Reduced Cost of Customer Acquisition. The outcome Increased Revenue is influenced positively by an outcome Increased Market Share. Both of these outcomes are realized by a combination of two principles: Serve Customers Wherever They Are and Serve Customers Whenever They Need Our Help. Both of these principles are realized by a combination of two requirements: Mobile Applications Shall Run On All Popular Mobile Platforms and Services Shall Be Accessible Through Mobile Browsers. The goal Reduced Cost Of Customer Acquisition is realized by a principle Respond To Changing Customer Needs, Preferences, And Expectations Quickly And Efficiently, which in turn is realized by a constraint Mobile Applications Shall Be Built With Cross-Platform Frameworks.

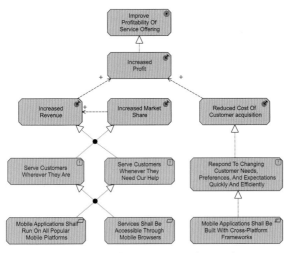

Example 18: Goal, Outcome, Principle, Requirement, and Constraint

5.3.3 Meaning and Value

Sending push notifications has a value of Cost Efficiency for the stakeholder Insurer, and a value of Being Informed and Peace of Mind (which is partly due to a value of Certainty) for the stakeholder Customer. Different meanings can be assigned to the different specific types of notification messages. A Confirmation Of Receipt Message has the meaning Claim Has Been Received, a Review Complete Message has the meaning Claim Review Complete, and a Payment Complete Message has the meaning Claim Has Been Paid.

5.4 Relationships with Core Elements

The purpose of the motivation elements is to model the motivation behind the core elements in an Enterprise Architecture. Therefore, it should be possible to relate motivation elements to core elements.

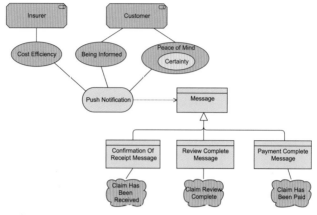

Example 19: Meaning and Value

As shown in Figure 22, a requirement (and, indirectly, also a principle, outcome, and goal) can be related directly to a structure or behavior element by means of a realization relationship. Also, the weaker influence relationship is allowed between these elements. Meaning and value can be associated with any structure or behavior element.

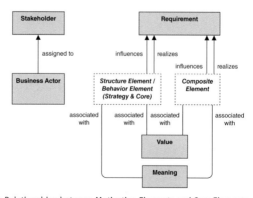

Figure 22: Relationships between Motivation Elements and Core Elements

Chapter 6
Strategy Elements

The strategy elements are used to model the capabilities of an organization, and how they are to be changed in order to achieve business outcomes.

6.1 Strategy Elements Metamodel
Figure 23 gives an overview of the strategy elements and their relationships.

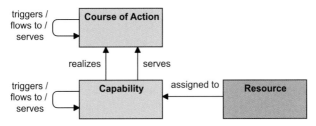

Figure 23: Strategy Elements Metamodel

6.2 Strategy Elements Summary
Table 6 gives an overview of the strategy elements, with their definitions.

6.3 Strategy Elements Example
Increase Profit is a goal that can be decomposed into a number of other goals: Decrease Costs and Increase Revenue. The former is related to the Operation Excellence strategy of the company, modeled as a course of action. This is decomposed into two other courses of action: Centralize IT Systems and Standardize Products. These result in two outcomes: Decreased Costs and Loss of Customers, which influence the goals in positive and negative ways. This shows an important difference between goals and outcomes: not all outcomes lead to the intended results.

Table 6: Strategy Elements

Element	Description	Notation
Resource	An asset owned or controlled by an individual or organization. Resources are a central concept in the field of strategic management, economics, computer science, portfolio management, and more. Resources can be classified into tangible assets – financial assets (e.g., cash, securities, borrowing capacity), physical assets (e.g., plant, equipment, land, mineral reserves), intangible assets (technology; e.g., patents, copyrights, trade secrets; reputation, e.g., brand, relationships; culture), and human assets (skills/know-how, capacity for communication and collaboration, motivation). The name of a resource should preferably be a noun.	Resource
Capability	An ability that an active structure element, such as an organization, person, or system, possesses. Capabilities focus on business outcomes. They provide a high-level view of the current and desired abilities of an organization, in relation to its strategy and its environment. They are realized by various elements (people, processes, systems, and so on) that can be described, designed, and implemented using Enterprise Architecture approaches. Capabilities may also have serving relationships, such as to denote that one capability contributes to another. Capabilities are often used for capability-based planning; i.e., to describe the evolution of capabilities over time. To model such so-called capability increments, the specialization relationship can be used to denote that a certain capability increment is a specific version of that capability.	Capability

Element	Description	Notation
Course of action	An approach or plan for configuring some capabilities and resources of the enterprise, undertaken to achieve a goal. A course of action represents what an enterprise has decided to do. Courses of action can be categorized as strategies and tactics. It is not possible to make a hard distinction between the two, but strategies tend to be long-term and fairly broad in scope, while tactics tend to shorter-term and narrower in scope.	Course of action

The courses of action are realized by a number of capabilities: IT Management & Operations and Product Management, and appropriate resources Human Resources and IT Resources are assigned to the former. The model fragment also shows that these resources are located in the Headquarters of the organization, in line with the Centralize IT Systems course of action.

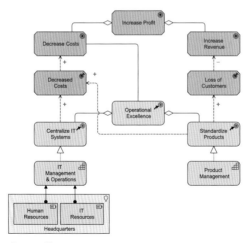

Example 20: Strategy Elements

6.4 Relationships with Motivation and Core Elements

Figure 24 shows how the strategy elements are related to core elements and motivation elements. Internal and external behavior elements may realize capabilities, while an active or passive structure element may realize a resource. Capabilities, courses of action, and resources may realize or influence requirements (and, indirectly, also principles or goals), and a course of action may also realize or influence an outcome (and, indirectly, also a goal).

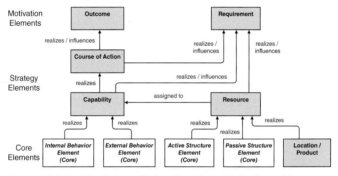

Figure 24: Relationships between Strategy Elements and Motivation and Core Elements

Chapter 7
Business Layer

The Business Layer is typically used (often in conjunction with the strategy elements described in Chapter 6) to model the business architecture of an enterprise that includes a description of the structure and interaction between the business strategy, organization, functions, business processes, and information needs.

7.1 Business Layer Metamodel

Figure 25 gives an overview of the Business Layer elements and their relationships. Business internal active structure element, business internal behavior element, and business passive structure element are abstract elements; only their specializations (as defined in the following sections) are instantiated in models.

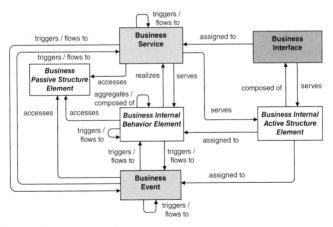

Figure 25: Business Layer Metamodel

7.2 Active Structure Elements

The active structure aspect of the Business Layer refers to the static structure of an organization, in terms of the entities that make up the organization and their relationships. The *active entities* are the subjects (e.g., business actors or business roles) that perform behavior such as business processes or functions (capabilities). Business actors may be individual persons (e.g., customers or employees), but also groups of people (organization units) and resources that have a permanent (or at least long-term) status within the organizations. Typical examples of the latter are a department and a business unit.

The element of business interface is introduced to explicitly model the (logical or physical) places or channels where the services that a role offers to the environment can be accessed. The same service may be offered on a number of different interfaces; e.g., by mail, by telephone, or through the Internet. In contrast to application modeling, it is uncommon in current Business Layer modeling approaches to recognize the business interface element.

In the Business Layer, three types of internal active structure element are defined: *business actor*, *business role*, and *business collaboration*.

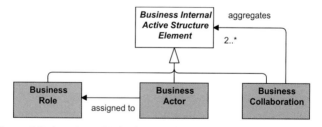

Figure 26: Business Internal Active Structure Elements

Table 7: Business Layer Active Structure Elements

Element	Description	Notation
Business actor	A business entity that is capable of performing behavior. A business actor is a business entity as opposed to a technical entity; i.e., it belongs to the Business Layer. Actors may, however, include entities outside the actual organization; e.g., customers and partners. A business actor may be assigned to one or more business roles. It can then perform the behavior to which these business roles are assigned. A business actor can be aggregated in a location. The name of a business actor should preferably be a noun.	Business actor
Business role	The responsibility for performing specific behavior, to which an actor can be assigned, or the part an actor plays in a particular action or event. Business roles with certain responsibilities or skills are assigned to business processes or business functions. A business role may be assigned to one or more business processes or business functions, while a business actor may be assigned to one or more business roles. The name of a business role should preferably be a noun.	Business role

Element	Description	Notation
Business collaboration	An aggregate of two or more business internal active structure elements that work together to perform collective behavior. A collaboration is a (possibly temporary) collection of business roles or actors within an organization, which perform collaborative behavior (interactions). The name of a business collaboration should preferably be a noun. It is also common to leave a business collaboration unnamed.	Business collaboration ⚭ ⚭
Business interface	A point of access where a business service is made available to the environment. A business interface exposes the functionality of a business service to other business roles or actors. It is often referred to as a channel (telephone, Internet, local office, etc.). The same business service may be exposed through different interfaces. The name of a business interface should preferably be a noun.	Business interface ─○ ─○

7.3 Behavior Elements

Based on service-orientation, a crucial design decision for the behavioral part of the ArchiMate metamodel is the distinction between "external" and "internal" behavior of an organization.

The externally visible behavior is modeled by the element *business service*. A distinction can be made between "external" business services, offered to external customers, and "internal" business services, offering supporting functionality to processes or functions within the organization.

Several types of internal behavior elements that can realize a service are distinguished: a *process view* and a *function view*; two elements associated with these views, *business process* and *business function*, are defined.

A *business interaction* is a unit of behavior similar to a business process or function, but which is performed in a collaboration of two or more roles within the organization.

A *business event* is something that happens (externally) and may influence business processes, functions, or interactions.

In the Business Layer, three types of internal behavior element are defined: business process, business function, and business interaction.

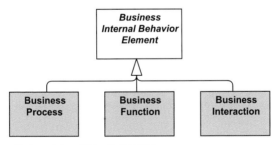

Figure 27: Business Internal Behavior Elements

7.4 Passive Structure Elements

The passive structure aspect at the Business Layer models the passive structure elements (business objects) that are manipulated by behavior, such as business processes or functions. The passive entities represent the important concepts in which the business thinks about a domain.

Table 8: Business Layer Behavior Elements

Element	Description	Notation
Business process	A sequence of business behaviors that achieves a specific outcome such as a defined set of products or business services. A business process describes the internal behavior performed by a business role that is required to produce a set of products and services. For a consumer, the products and services are relevant and the behavior is merely a black box, hence the designation "internal". The name of a business process should clearly indicate a predefined sequence of actions, and may include the word "process".	Business process
Business function	A collection of business behavior based on a chosen set of criteria (typically required business resources and/or competences), closely aligned to an organization, but not necessarily explicitly governed by the organization. Like a business process, a business function also describes internal behavior performed by a business role. However, while a business process groups behavior based on a sequence or flow of activities that is needed to realize a product or service, a business function typically groups behavior based on required business resources, skills, competences, knowledge, etc. The name of a business function should clearly indicate a well-defined behavior.	Business function

Element	Description	Notation
Business interaction	A unit of collective business behavior performed by (a collaboration of) two or more business roles. A business interaction is similar to a business process/function, but while a process/function may be performed by a single role, an interaction is performed by a collaboration of multiple roles. The roles in the collaboration share the responsibility for performing the interaction. The name of a business interaction should preferably be a verb in the simple present tense.	Business interaction
Business event	A business behavior element that denotes an organizational state change. It may originate from and be resolved inside or outside the organization. Business processes and other business behavior may be triggered or interrupted by a business event. Also, business processes may raise events that trigger other business processes, functions, or interactions. Unlike business processes, functions, and interactions, a business event is instantaneous: it does not have duration. The name of a business event should preferably be a verb in the perfect tense; e.g., claim received.	Business event

Element	Description	Notation
Business service	An explicitly defined exposed business behavior. A business service exposes the functionality of business roles or collaborations to their environment. This functionality is accessed through one or more business interfaces. The name of a business service should preferably be a verb ending with "ing"; e.g., transaction processing. Also, a name explicitly containing the word "service" may be used.	

In the Business Layer, there are two main types of passive structure elements: business object and representation. Furthermore, a contract, used in the context of a product, is a specialization of a business object.

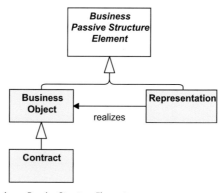

Figure 28: Business Passive Structure Elements

Table 9: Business Layer Passive Structure Elements

Element	Description	Notation
Business object	A concept used within a particular business domain. A business object typically models an object type (*cf.* a UML class) of which multiple instances may exist in operations. Only occasionally, business objects represent actual instances of information produced and consumed by behavior elements such as business processes. This is in particular the case for singleton types; i.e., types that have only one instance. The name of a business object is preferably a noun.	Business object
Contract	A formal or informal specification of an agreement between a provider and a consumer that specifies the rights and obligations associated with a product and establishes functional and non-functional parameters for interaction. The contract element may be used to model a contract in the legal sense, but also a more informal agreement associated with a product. It may also be or include a Service-Level Agreement (SLA), describing an agreement about the functionality and quality of the services that are part of a product. A contract is a specialization of a business object. The name of a contract is preferably a noun.	Contract

Element	Description	Notation
Representation	A perceptible form of the information carried by a business object. Representations (for example, messages or documents) are the perceptible carriers of information that are related to business objects. If relevant, representations can be classified in various ways; for example, in terms of medium (electronic, paper, audio, etc.) or format (HTML, ASCII, PDF, RTF, etc.). The name of a representation is preferably a noun.	Representation

7.5 Composite Elements

The Business Layer contains one composite element: product. This aggregates or composes services and passive structure elements across the layers of the ArchiMate core language.

Table 10: Business Layer Composite Elements

Element	Description	Notation
Product	A coherent collection of services and/or passive structure elements, accompanied by a contract/set of agreements, which is offered as a whole to (internal or external) customers. This covers both intangible, services-based, or information products that are common in information-intensive organizations, and tangible, physical products. "Buying" a product gives the customer the right to use the associated services. The name of a product is usually the name which is used in the communication with customers, or possibly a more generic noun (e.g., "travel insurance").	Product

7.6 Examples

7.6.1 Business Active Structure Elements

The ArchiSurance Contact Center, modeled as a business actor, is composed of three employees, also modeled as business actors: Greg, Joan, and Larry. The Contact Center has three business interfaces to serve customers: Phone, E-mail, and Web Chat. Greg fulfills the business role of Travel Insurance Claim Analyst, Joan fulfills the business role of Home Insurance Product Specialist, and Larry fulfills the business role of Customer Service Representative. The former two business roles are specializations of a business role Specialist. High-Risk Claims Adjudication is a business collaboration of two business roles: Specialist and Customer Service Representative.

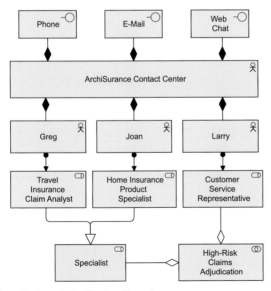

Example 21: Business Active Structure Elements

7.6.2 Business Behavior Elements

Claims Administration is a business function that is composed of a
number of business processes and a business interaction. This business
function realizes a Claims Processing business service. A business event
Claim Filed triggers the first business process, Accept Claim, which
in turn triggers a business process Assign Claim. Depending on the
type of claim, either the business process Adjudicate Standard Claim
or the business interaction Adjudicate High-Risk Claim is performed.
Adjudication of high-risk claims is a business interaction because,
according to the company policy, two people should always be involved
in this activity to minimize the risk of fraud. After adjudication, the
business processes Notify Customer and Pay Claim are performed in
parallel, and when both have finished, business process Close Claim is
triggered.

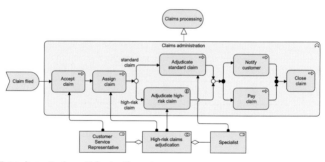

Example 22: Business Behavior Elements

7.6.3 Business Passive Structure Elements

Business object Claim may be realized by either of the following three
physical representations (in different stages of the Claims Administration
process): Submission Form, Claim File Summary, or Claim Letter. All
of these representations refer to a representation Policy Summary, which
realizes a contract Insurance Policy.

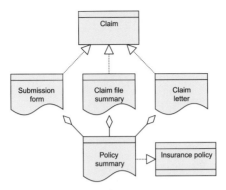

Example 23: Business Passive Structure Elements

7.6.4 Business Composite Element: Product

A product Insurance consists of a contract Insurance Policy and a
business service Customer Service, which aggregates four other business
services: Application, Renewal, Claims Processing, and Appeal. An
Auto Insurance product is a specialization of the generic Insurance
product, with an additional business service Drive Well and Save, and
accompanying contract Drive Well and Save Agreement.

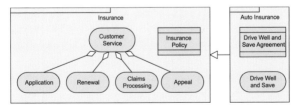

Example 24: Business Composite Element: Product

Chapter 8
Application Layer

The Application Layer is typically used to model the information systems architectures of the enterprise, including the application architecture that describes the structure and interaction of the applications.

8.1 Application Layer Metamodel
Figure 29 gives an overview of the Application Layer elements and their relationships. Whenever applicable, inspiration has been drawn from the analogy with the Business Layer.

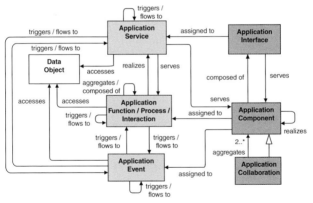

Figure 29: Application Layer Metamodel

8.2 Active Structure Elements
The main active structure element for the Application Layer is the *application component*. This concept is used to model any structural entity in the Application Layer. It can describe (re-usable) software components that can be part of one or more applications, and also complete software applications, sub-applications, or information systems.

The *application collaboration* element is introduced here as the inter-relationships of components are important in an application architecture. It is defined as a collection of application components which perform application interactions.

An *application interface* is the (logical) channel through which the services of a component can be accessed. The application interface concept can be used to model both *application-to-application* interfaces, which offer internal application services, and *application-to business* interfaces (and/or *user interfaces*), which offer external application services.

Table 11: Application Layer – Active Structure Elements

Element	Definition	Notation
Application component	An encapsulation of application functionality aligned to implementation structure, which is modular and replaceable. It encapsulates its behavior and data, exposes services, and makes them available through interfaces. An application component is a self-contained unit. As such, it is independently deployable, re-usable, and replaceable. An application component performs one or more application functions. The name of an application component should preferably be a noun.	Application component

Element	Definition	Notation
Application collaboration	An aggregate of two or more application components that work together to perform collective application behavior. An application collaboration specifies which components cooperate to perform some task. The collaborative behavior, including, for example, the communication pattern of these components, is modeled by an application interaction. An application collaboration typically models a logical or temporary collaboration of application components, and does not exist as a separate entity in the enterprise. The name of an application collaboration should preferably be a noun.	Application collaboration
Application interface	A point of access where application services are made available to a user, another application component, or a node. An application interface specifies how the functionality of a component can be accessed by other elements. An application interface exposes application services to the environment. The same application service may be exposed through different interfaces, and the same interface may expose multiple services. The name of an application interface should preferably be a noun.	Application interface

8.3 Behavior Elements

Behavior in the Application Layer is described in a similar way to Business Layer behavior. A distinction is made between the external behavior of application components in terms of *application services*, and the internal behavior of these components; i.e., *application functions* that realize these services.

An *application service* is an externally visible unit of functionality, provided by one or more components, exposed through well-defined interfaces, and meaningful to the environment. The functionality that an interactive computer program provides through a user interface is also modeled using an application service, exposed by an application-to-business interface representing the user interface. Internal application services are exposed through an application-to-application interface.

An *application function* describes the internal behavior of a component needed to realize one or more application services. An *application process* models an ordering of application behavior, as a counterpart of a business process.

An *application interaction* is the behavior of a collaboration of two or more application components. An application interaction is external behavior from the perspective of each of the participating components, but the behavior is internal to the collaboration as a whole.

8.4 Passive Structure Concepts

The passive counterpart of the application component in the Application Layer is called a *data object*. A data object is a representation of a business object, as a counterpart of the representation element in the Business Layer.

Table 12: Application Layer – Behavior Elements

Element	Definition	Notation
Application function	Automated behavior that can be performed by an application component. An application function describes the internal behavior of an application component. If this behavior is exposed externally, this is done through one or more services. The name of an application function should preferably be a verb ending with "ing"; e.g., "accounting".	
Application interaction	A unit of collective application behavior performed by (a collaboration of) two or more application components. An application interaction describes the collective behavior that is performed by the components that participate in an application collaboration. An application interaction can also specify the externally visible behavior needed to realize an application service. The name of an application interaction should clearly identify a series of application behaviors; e.g., "Client profile creation" or "Update customer records".	

Element	Definition	Notation
Application process	A sequence of application behaviors that achieves a specific outcome. An application process describes the internal behavior performed by an application component that is required to realize a set of services. For a (human or automated) consumer the services are relevant and the required behavior is merely a black box, hence the designation "internal". The name of an application process should clearly identify a series of application behaviors; e.g., "Claims adjudication process", or "General ledger update job".	Application process
Application event	An application behavior element that denotes a state change. Application functions and other application behavior may be triggered or interrupted by an application event. Also, application behavior may raise events that trigger other application behavior. Unlike processes, functions, and interactions, an event is instantaneous; it does not have duration. Events may originate from the environment of the organization (e.g., from an external application), but also internal events may occur generated by, for example, other applications within the organization. The name of an application event should preferably be a verb in the perfect tense; e.g., "claim received".	Application event

Element	Definition	Notation
Application service	An explicitly defined exposed application behavior. An application service exposes the functionality of components to their environment. This functionality is accessed through one or more application interfaces. An application service is realized by one or more application functions that are performed by the component. It may require, use, and produce data objects. The name of an application service should preferably be a verb ending with "ing"; e.g., "transaction processing". Also, a name explicitly containing the word "service" may be used.	Application service

Table 13: Application Layer – Passive Structure Element

Element	Definition	Notation
Data object	Data structured for automated processing. A data object should be a self-contained piece of information with a clear meaning to the business, not just to the application level. Typical examples of data objects are a customer record, a client database, or an insurance claim. The name of a data object should preferably be a noun.	Data object

8.5 Examples

8.5.1 Application Active Structure Elements

The Online Travel Insurance Sales application collaboration aggregates two application components: Quotation and Purchase. The application collaboration provides an application interface Web Services Interface that serves another application component Travel Website.

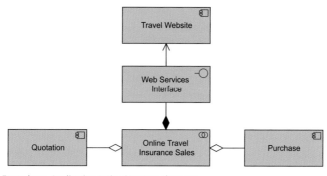

Example 25: Application Active Structure Elements

8.5.2 Application Behavior Elements

The Purchase Travel Insurance application interaction is composed of two application functions: Prepare Quotation, realizing an application service Get Quotation, and Finalize Purchase, realizing an application service Purchase Quoted Insurance. This application interaction models the cooperative behavior of the Quotation and Purchase application components, modeled as the application collaboration Online Travel Insurance Sales in Example 24. An application event Request for a Quotation triggers an application process Obtain Travel Insurance, which is served by the two aforementioned application services.

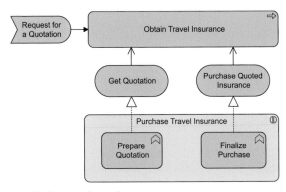

Example 26: Application Behavior Elements

8.5.3 Application Passive Structure Elements

An Online Insurance Quotation data object is composed of three other data objects: Quoted Price, Terms and Conditions, and Certificate of Authenticity. Auto Insurance Quotation and Travel Insurance Quotation are two specializations of the Online Insurance Quotation data object. Travel Insurance Quotation contains an additional data object Purchased Itinerary.

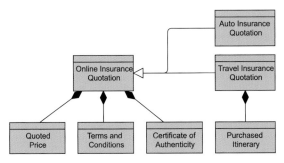

Example 27: Application Passive Structure Elements

Chapter 9
Technology Layer

The Technology Layer is typically used to model the technology architecture of the enterprise including the structure and interaction of the platform services, and logical and physical technology components.

9.1 Technology Layer Metamodel

Figure 30 gives an overview of the Technology Layer elements and their relationships. Whenever applicable, inspiration is drawn from the analogy with the Business and Application Layers.

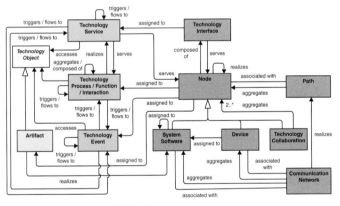

Figure 30: Technology Layer Metamodel

9.2 Active Structure Elements

The main active structure element for the Technology Layer is the *node*. This element is used to model structural entities in this layer. A *technology interface* is the (logical) place where the technology services offered by a node can be accessed by other nodes or by application components from the Application Layer.

The inter-relationships of components in the Technology Layer are mainly formed by the communication infrastructure. The *path* models the relation between two or more nodes, through which these nodes can exchange information. The physical realization of a path is modeled with a *communication network*; i.e., a physical communication medium between two or more devices (or other networks).

Table 14: Technology Layer – Active Structure Elements

Element	Definition	Notation
Node	A computational or physical resource that hosts, manipulates, or interacts with other computational or physical resources. Nodes are active structure elements that perform technology behavior and execute, store, and process technology objects such as artifacts (or materials). Nodes can be interconnected by paths. The name of a node should preferably be a noun.	Node

Element	Definition	Notation
Device	A physical IT resource upon which system software and artifacts may be stored or deployed for execution. A device is a specialization of a node that represents a physical IT resource with processing capability. It is typically used to model hardware systems such as mainframes, PCs, or routers. Usually, they are part of a node together with system software. Devices may be composite; i.e., consist of sub-devices. The name of a device should preferably be a noun referring to the type of hardware; e.g., "IBM System z mainframe".	Device
System software	Software that provides or contributes to an environment for storing, executing, and using software or data deployed within it. System software is a specialization of a node that is used to model the software environment in which artifacts run. This can be, for example, an operating system, a JEE application server, a database system, or a workflow engine.	System software

Element	Definition	Notation
Technology collaboration	An aggregate of two or more nodes that work together to perform collective technology behavior. A technology collaboration specifies which nodes cooperate to perform some task. The collaborative behavior, including, for example, the communication pattern of these nodes, is modeled by a technology interaction. A technology collaboration typically models a logical or temporary collaboration of nodes, and does not exist as a separate entity in the enterprise. The name of a technology collaboration should preferably be a noun.	Technology collaboration
Technology interface	A point of access where technology services offered by a node can be accessed. A technology interface specifies how the technology services of a node can be accessed by other nodes. A technology interface exposes a technology service to the environment. The same service may be exposed through different interfaces. The name of a technology interface should preferably be a noun.	Technology interface

Element	Definition	Notation
Path	A link between two or more nodes, through which these nodes can exchange data or material. A path is used to model the logical communication (or distribution) relations between nodes. It is realized by one or more communication networks (or distribution networks when modeling physical elements), which represent the physical communication (or distribution) links. The properties (e.g., bandwidth, latency) of a path are usually aggregated from these underlying networks.	Path ⟨·⟩ ⟨··▷
Communication network	A set of structures that connects computer systems or other electronic devices for transmission, routing, and reception of data or data-based communications such as voice and video. A communication network represents the physical communication infrastructure.	Communication network ↔

9.3 Behavior Elements

Behavior elements in the Technology Layer are similar to the behavior elements in the other two layers. A distinction is made between the external behavior of nodes in terms of *technology services*, and the internal behavior of these nodes; i.e., *technology functions* that realize these services.

Table 15: Technology Layer – Behavior Elements

Element	Definition	Notation
Technology function	A collection of technology behavior that can be performed by a node. A technology function describes the internal behavior of a node; for the user of a node that performs a technology function, this function is invisible. If its behavior is exposed externally, this is done through one or more technology services.	Technology function
Technology process	A sequence of technology behaviors that achieves a specific outcome. A technology process describes internal behavior of a node; for the user of that node, this process is invisible. If its behavior is exposed externally, this is done through one or more technology services. The name of a technology process should clearly identify a series of technology behaviors; e.g., "System boot sequence" or "Replicate database".	Technology process

Element	Definition	Notation
Technology interaction	A unit of collective technology behavior performed by (a collaboration of) two or more nodes. A technology interaction describes the collective behavior that is performed by the nodes that participate in a technology collaboration. This may, for example, include the communication pattern between these components. A technology interaction can also specify the externally visible behavior needed to realize a technology service. The name of a technology interaction should clearly identify a series of technology behaviors; e.g., "Client profile creation" or "Update customer records".	Technology interaction
Technology event	A technology behavior element that denotes a state change. Technology functions and other technology behavior may be triggered or interrupted by a technology event. Also, technology functions may raise events that trigger other infrastructure behavior. Unlike processes, functions, and interactions, an event is instantaneous: it does not have duration. The name of a technology event should preferably be a verb in the perfect tense; e.g., "message received".	Technology event

Element	Definition	Notation
Technology service	An explicitly defined exposed technology behavior. A technology service exposes the functionality of a node to its environment. This functionality is accessed through one or more technology interfaces. It may require, use, and produce artifacts. The name of a technology service should preferably be a verb ending with "ing"; e.g., "messaging". Also, a name explicitly containing the word "service" may be used.	

9.4 Passive Structure Elements

A technology object represents a passive element that is used or produced by technology behavior. Technology objects represent the "physical" objects manipulated by the infrastructure of an enterprise. Technology objects are abstract elements; i.e., they are not instantiated in models but serve as the generic type of the things manipulated by the Technology Layer. This may include both artifacts (e.g., files) and physical material.

An *artifact* is a physical piece of information that is used or produced in a software development process, or by deployment and operation of a system.

Table 16: Technology Layer – Passive Structure Elements

Artifact	A piece of data that is used or produced in a software development process, or by deployment and operation of a system. An artifact represents a tangible element in the IT world. Artifact is a specialization of technology object. It is typically used to model (software) products such as source files, executables, scripts, database tables, messages, documents, specifications, and model files. An instance (copy) of an artifact can be deployed on a node. An artifact could be used to represent a physical data component that realizes a data object. The name of an artifact should preferably be the name of the file it represents; e.g., "order.jar".	Artifact

9.5 Examples

9.5.1 Technology Active Structure Elements

Two Blade System devices are connected to a communication network Data Center Network. This in turn is connected to another communication network Wide Area Network through a node Data Center Switch. The two communication networks together realize a path Data Replication Path. Both Blade System devices and the Data Center Switch node have a technology interface Management Interface. Device Blade System 1 deploys Hypervisor system software for hardware virtualization. Two system software components are deployed on the Hypervisor: an Open Source Operating System and a Proprietary Operating System, creating two virtual hosts, modeled as nodes Quotation Virtual Host and Purchase Virtual Host.

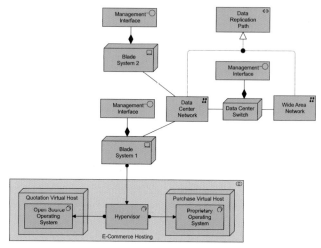

Example 28: Technology Active Structure Elements

9.5.2 Technology Behavior Elements

A technology event Database Update triggers a technology process
Remote Data Replication, which is served by a technology service
Replicate Database Updates. This technology service is realized by
a technology function Database Replication, which is composed of
four other technology functions: Administrate Replication, Handle
Local Updates, Handle Remote Updates, and Monitor Replication
Status. There are information flows from the Administrate Replication
technology function to the other three technology functions.

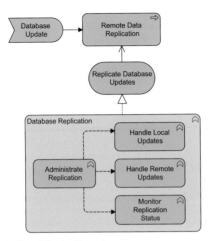

Example 29: Technology Behavior Elements

9.5.3 Technology Passive Structure Element: Artifact

A Web Archive artifact (which may realize an application component) is composed of two other artifacts: Database Access Java Archive and Business Logic Java Archive. Two specializations of the Web Archive artifact are a Purchase Application Web Archive and a Quotation Application Web Archive. A Travel Insurance Database artifact (which may realize a data object) is associated with the Web Archive artifact.

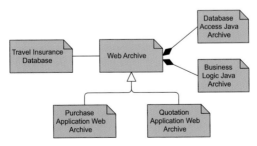

Example 30: Technology Passive Structure Element: Artifact

Chapter 10
Physical Elements

The physical elements are added as an extension to the Technology Layer for modeling the physical world.

10.1 Physical Elements Metamodel

Figure 31 gives an overview of the physical elements and their relationships. These are based on the Technology Layer.

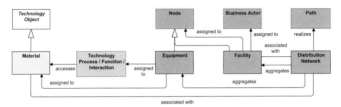

Figure 31: Physical Elements Metamodel

10.2 Active Structure Elements

The *equipment* element is the main active structure element within the physical elements. It is used to model any physical machinery, tools, instruments, or implements.

The inter-relationships of physical elements are mainly formed by the logistics infrastructure. The path element from the Technology Layer models the relation between two or more nodes, through which these nodes can exchange information or material. The physical realization of a path is modeled with a *distribution network*; i.e., a physical connection between two or more pieces of equipment (or other physical networks). This can be used to model, for example, rail or road networks, the water supply, power grid, or gas network.

Table 17: Physical Elements – Active Structure

Element	Definition	Notation
Equipment	One or more physical machines, tools, or instruments that can create, use, store, move, or transform materials. Equipment comprises all active processing elements that carry out physical processes in which materials (which are a special kind of technology object) are used or transformed. Equipment is a specialization of the node element from the Technology Layer. Therefore, it is possible to model nodes that are formed by a combination of IT infrastructure (devices, system software) and physical infrastructure (equipment); e.g., an MRI scanner at a hospital, a production plant with its control systems, etc. The name of a piece of equipment should preferably be a noun.	Equip-ment

Element	Definition	Notation
Facility	A physical structure or environment. A facility is a specialization of a node. It represents a physical resource that has the capability of facilitating (e.g., housing or locating) the use of equipment. It is typically used to model factories, buildings, or outdoor constructions that have an important role in production or distribution processes. Examples of facilities include a factory, a laboratory, a warehouse, a shopping mall, a cave, or a spaceship. Facilities may be composite; i.e., consist of sub-facilities. The name of a facility should preferably be a noun referring to the type of facility; e.g., "Rotterdam harbor oil refinery".	Facility
Distribution network	A physical network used to transport materials or energy. A distribution network represents the physical distribution or transportation infrastructure. It embodies the physical realization of the logical paths between nodes.	Distribution network ⇔

10.3 Behavior Elements

No separate physical behavior elements are defined. The behavior elements from the Technology Layer (technology function, process, interaction, service, and event) are used to model the behavior of all nodes, including physical equipment. Since equipment will very often be computer-controlled or in other ways have a close relationship to IT (e.g., Internet of Things), their behavior can be described in an integral way using the existing technology behavior concepts.

10.4 Passive Structure Elements

Table 18: Physical Elements – Passive Structure

Element	Definition	Notation
Material	Tangible physical matter or physical elements. Material represents tangible physical matter, with attributes such as size and weight. It is typically used to model raw materials and physical products, and also energy sources such as fuel. Material can be accessed by physical processes. The name of material should be a noun.	Material

10.5 Physical Elements Example

An Assembly Line, modeled as equipment, and installed at a facility Manufacturing Plant, makes use of materials Pre-Assembled Circuit Board, Internal Antenna, and Plastic Case to produce material Vehicle Telematics Appliance. The appliance, initially located at the Manufacturing Plant facility, is subsequently transported to the facilities National Distribution Center and Local Distribution Center, making use of the distribution networks Overseas Shipping and Local Trucking. These distribution networks together realize the path Intermodal Freight.

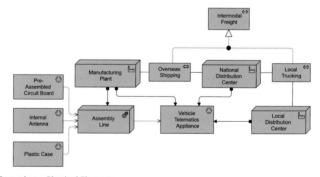

Example 31: Physical Elements

Chapter 11
Cross-Layer Dependencies

A central issue in Enterprise Architecture is business-IT alignment: how can the Business, Application, and Technology Layers be matched? This chapter describes the relationships that the ArchiMate language offers to model the link between business, applications, and technology.

11.1 Alignment of Business Layer and Lower Layers

Figure 32 shows the relationships between the Business Layer, the Application Layer, and the Technology Layer elements. There are two main types of relationships between these layers:

1. *Serving* relationships, between application service and the different types of business behavior elements, and between application interface and business role; *vice versa*, serving relationships between business service and application behavior elements, and between business interface and application component. These relationships represent the behavioral and structural aspects of the support of the business by applications.

2. *Realization* relationships, from an application process or function to a business process or function, or from a data object or a technology object to a business object, to indicate that the data object is a digital representation of the corresponding business object, or the technology object is a physical representation of the business object.

In addition, there may be an aggregation relationship between a product and an application or technology service, and a data or technology object, to indicate that these services or objects can be offered directly to a customer as part of the product.

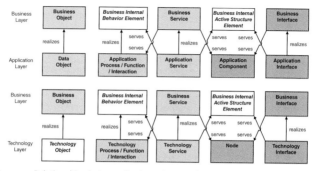

Figure 32: Relationships between Business Layer and Application and Technology Layer Elements

11.2 Alignment of Application and Technology Layers

Figure 33 shows the relationships between Application Layer and Technology Layer elements. There are two types of relationships between these layers:

1. *Serving* relationships, between technology service and the different types of application behavior elements, and between technology interface and application component; *vice versa*, serving relationships between application service and technology behavior, and application interface and node. These relationships represent the behavioral and structural aspects of the use of technology infrastructure by applications and *vice versa*.

2. *Realization* relationships from technology process or function to application process or function, from technology object to data object, to indicate that the data object is realized by, for example, a physical data file, from technology object to application component, to indicate that a physical data file is an executable that realizes an application or part of an application. (Note: In this case, an artifact represents a "physical" component that is deployed on a node; this is modeled with an assignment relationship. A (logical) application component is

realized by an artifact and, indirectly, by the node on which the
artifact is deployed.)

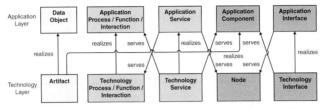

Figure 33: Relationships between Application Layer and Technology Layer Elements

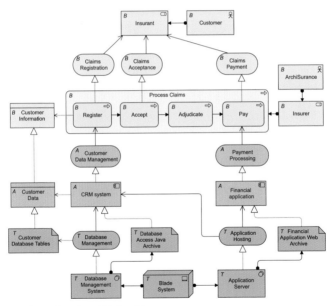

Example 32: Cross-Layer Relationships

Due to derived relationships, it is also possible to draw relationships directly between the Business and Technology Layers. For example, if a business object is realized by a data object, which in turn is realized by a technology object, this technology object indirectly realizes the business object.

11.3 Cross-Layer Relationships Example

Example 31 shows how the cross-layer relationships integrate the different layers, and how you can depict this in one view. It also shows how the optional notation with letters in the upper-left corner is used to distinguish between layers.

Chapter 12
Implementation and Migration Elements

The implementation and migration elements support the implementation and migration of architectures. This includes concepts for modeling implementation programs and projects to support program, portfolio, and project management, and a plateau concept to support migration planning.

12.1 Implementation and Migration Elements Metamodel

Figure 34 gives an overview of the implementation and migration elements and their relationships.

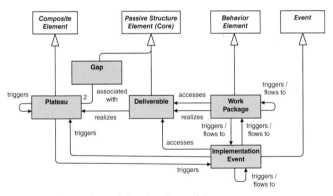

Figure 34: Implementation and Migration Metamodel

12.2 Implementation and Migration Elements

The central behavioral concept is a *work package*. A work package is a behavior element that has a clearly defined beginning and end date, and

a well-defined set of goals or results. The work package concept can be
used at many levels to model projects, sub-projects, or tasks within a
project, program, or project portfolio.

Work packages produce *deliverables*. These may be results of any kind,
such as reports, papers, services, software, physical products, etc., or
intangible results such as organizational change. A deliverable may also
be the implementation of (a part of) an architecture.

Work packages may be triggered or interrupted by an *implementation
event*. Also, work packages may raise events that trigger other behavior.
Unlike a work package, an event is instantaneous: it does not have
duration.

The *plateau* element is included to support the different states of an
architecture in the TOGAF framework, namely the Baseline, Target, and
Transition Architecture states.

A *gap* is an outcome of the gap analysis technique, and forms an
important input for the implementation and migration planning.
The gap element is linked to two plateaus (e.g., Baseline and Target
Architecture, or two subsequent Transition Architectures), and represents
the differences between these plateaus.

Table 19: Implementation and Migration Elements

Element	Definition	Notation
Work package	A series of actions identified and designed to achieve specific results within specified time and resource constraints.	Work package
Deliverable	A precisely-defined outcome of a work package.	Deliverable

Element	Definition	Notation
Implementation event	A behavior element that denotes a state change related to implementation or migration. The name of an implementation event should preferably be a verb in the perfect tense; e.g., "project initiation phase completed".	Implementation event
Plateau	A relatively stable state of the architecture that exists during a limited period of time.	Plateau
Gap	A statement of difference between two plateaus.	Gap

12.3 Implementation and Migration Elements Example

The Next Generation Services Program work package is composed of three other work packages. An implementation event Program Approved triggers the first work package, Architecture And Planning, which triggers the work package Application Services Layer Development, which triggers the work package Business Services Development, which triggers the implementation event Program Completed. The Program Approved implementation event also provides a deliverable Program Brief, as input for the first work package. Work package Architecture And Planning realizes three deliverables: Business Plan, Architecture, and Roadmap (which is accessed by the Application Services Layer Development work package), which collectively realize the plateau Strategic Plan Complete. This plateau follows the initial plateau Baseline, filling the gap Knowledge Of How To Address Customer Needs. Similarly, the other work packages realize other deliverables that realize the subsequent plateaus.

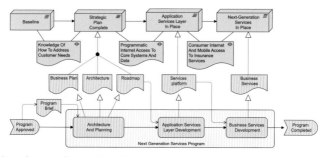

Example 33: Implementation and Migration Elements

12.4 Relationships

The implementation and migration elements use the standard ArchiMate relationships.

12.5 Cross-Aspect Dependencies

Figure 35 shows how the implementation and migration elements can be related to the ArchiMate core elements.

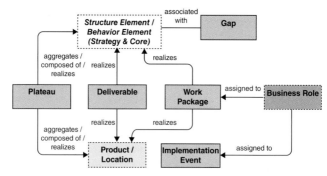

Figure 35: Relationships of Implementation and Migration Elements with Core Elements

Chapter 13
ArchiMate Viewpoints

The ArchiMate language provides a flexible approach in which architects and other stakeholders can use their own views on the Enterprise Architecture. In this approach, views are specified by viewpoints. Viewpoints define abstractions on the set of models representing the Enterprise Architecture, each aimed at a particular type of stakeholder and addressing a particular set of concerns. Viewpoints can be used to view certain aspects in isolation, and to relate two or more aspects.

13.1 Views and Viewpoints

Views are an ideal mechanism to purposefully convey information about architecture areas. In general, a view is defined as a part of an Architecture Description that addresses a set of related concerns and is tailored for specific stakeholders. A view is specified by means of a viewpoint, which prescribes the concepts, models, analysis techniques, and visualizations that are provided by the view. Simply put, a view is what you see and a viewpoint is where you are looking from.

Viewpoints are a means to focus on particular aspects and layers of the architecture. These aspects and layers are determined by the concerns of a stakeholder with whom communication takes place. What should and should not be visible from a specific viewpoint is therefore entirely dependent on the argumentation with respect to a stakeholder's concerns.

13.2 Viewpoint Mechanism

An architect is confronted with many different types of stakeholders and concerns. To help him in selecting the right viewpoints for the task at hand, the standard introduces a framework for the definition and classification of viewpoints, the viewpoint mechanism. The framework is based on two dimensions: purpose and content. Figure 36 shows how the viewpoint mechanism is used to create views addressing stakeholder concerns.

The architect communicates with the stakeholder to understand and document their concerns. The viewpoint mechanism is used to identify purpose and content and to help define and classify the viewpoint. The viewpoint governs the construction and design of the view. The view is a description of the architecture addressing stakeholder concerns and is governed by the viewpoint.

An example set of viewpoints is provided in the ArchiMate 3.0.1 Specification.

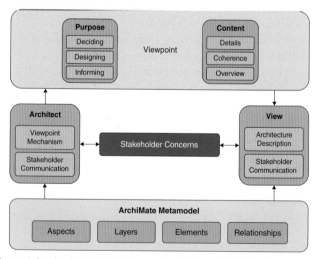

Figure 36: Framing Stakeholder Concerns using the Viewpoint Mechanism

Appendix A
Changes from Version 2.1 to Version 3.0

The main changes between Version 2.1 and Version 3.0 of the ArchiMate Specification are listed below.[2] Note that this is not an exhaustive list; various smaller improvements have been made throughout the text of the specification.

- Changed various definitions to increase alignment with the TOGAF framework
- Added an upper-level generic metamodel to explain the full structure of the language
- Restructured the set of relationships into structural, dynamic, dependency, and other relationships
- Allowed relationships to other relationships in some cases; e.g., to associate objects with flows or aggregate relationships within plateaus
- Improved the derivation of relationships, relaxed the constraints on relationships between layers in the ArchiMate core language, and improved the grouping and junction concepts
- Renamed the 'used by' relationship to 'serving', in line with the other active names of relationships
- Changed the notation of the influence relationship for consistency with the other dependency relationships (access and serving)
- Introduced a directional notation for the assignment relationship by replacing the black circle at the 'to' end by an arrow

---

2 For details of the changes between Version 3.0 and Version 3.0.1, see ArchiMate® Version 3.0: Technical Corrigendum No. 1 (U172), published by The Open Group, August 2017; www.opengroup. org/bookstore/catalog/u172.htm

- Added an optional notation to denote the layer of an element; a letter 'M', 'S', 'B', 'A', 'T', 'P', or 'I' in the top-left corner of an element can be used to denote a Motivation, Strategy, Business, Application, Technology, Physical, or Implementation & Migration element, respectively
- Changed the notation of the representation and contract elements, to distinguish these from deliverable and business object, respectively
- Added events (with a time attribute) at all layers in the ArchiMate core language as well as to the implementation and migration elements
- Renamed the Motivation Extension to motivation elements and introduced a new outcome element
- Moved the value and meaning concepts from the Business Layer of the ArchiMate core language to the motivation elements
- Introduced new strategy elements for modeling the enterprise at a strategic level, notably capability, resource, and course of action
- Moved the location element to the generic metamodel chapter
- Abolished the 'required interface' notation
- Renamed the elements in the Technology Layer from infrastructure x to technology x
- Added application process, technology process , technology interaction, and technology collaboration, to increase the regularity of the layers
- Extended the Technology Layer with elements for modeling the physical world: facility, equipment, material, and distribution network
- Renamed the 'communication path' element to 'path' and extended its meaning, to integrate with the physical elements
- Improved the description of viewpoints and the viewpoints mechanism, removed the introductory viewpoint, and moved the basic viewpoints listed in the standard to an informative appendix to indicate they are intended as examples, not as a normative or exhaustive list
- Replaced the examples throughout the specification
- Added a new appendix describing the relationship of the ArchiMate Specification to a number of other standards

- Created new tables of relationships based on the changes in the metamodel and derivation properties

ArchiMate 2.1 models are still mostly valid in Version 3.0. Two transformations should be applied to ensure conformance to the new version of the standard:
- Rename 'used by' relationships to 'serving'
- If a relationship between two elements in a model is no longer permitted, replace it by an association

If it concerns an assignment of an application component to a business process or function, this may be replaced by a realization relationship from the application component to the business process or function. If it concerns an assignment of a location to another element, this may be replaced by an aggregation. In some cases, the modeler may want to replace the location by a facility.

Glossary

ArchiMate Core Framework
A reference structure used to classify elements of the ArchiMate core language. It consists of three layers and three aspects.

ArchiMate Core Language
The central part of the ArchiMate language that defines the concepts and relationships to model Enterprise Architectures. It includes concepts from three layers: Business, Application, and Technology.

Aspect
Classification of elements based on layer-independent characteristics related to the concerns of different stakeholders. Used for positioning elements in the ArchiMate metamodel.

Attribute
A property associated with an ArchiMate language element or relationship.

Concept
Either an element or a relationship.

Conformance
Fulfillment of specified requirements.

Conforming Implementation
An implementation which satisfies the conformance requirements defined by the conformance clause of the standard.

Core Element
A structure or behavior element in one of the core layers of the ArchiMate language.

Composite Element
An element consisting of other elements from multiple aspects or layers of the language.

Element
Basic unit in the ArchiMate metamodel. Used to define and describe the constituent parts of Enterprise Architectures and their unique set of characteristics.

Layer
An abstraction of the ArchiMate Framework at which an enterprise can be modeled.

Model
A collection of concepts in the context of the ArchiMate language structure.
For a general definition of model, refer to the TOGAF framework.

Relationship
A connection between a source and target concept. Classified as structural, dependency, dynamic, or other.

Index